EMPTY AIR CLEAN ENERGY
悟空 悟能 悟净

by
David Chen
南郭求败

Empty Air Clean Energy

悟空 悟能 悟净

ISBN: 978-0-9861612-4-7

Copyright: Empty Air Clean Energy LLC, 2018

空气能源净化环保公司 · 版权所有 · 2018

Claim the Earth series

《玩世》系列丛书

De Revolutionibus Orbium Coelestium

一阴一阳之谓道

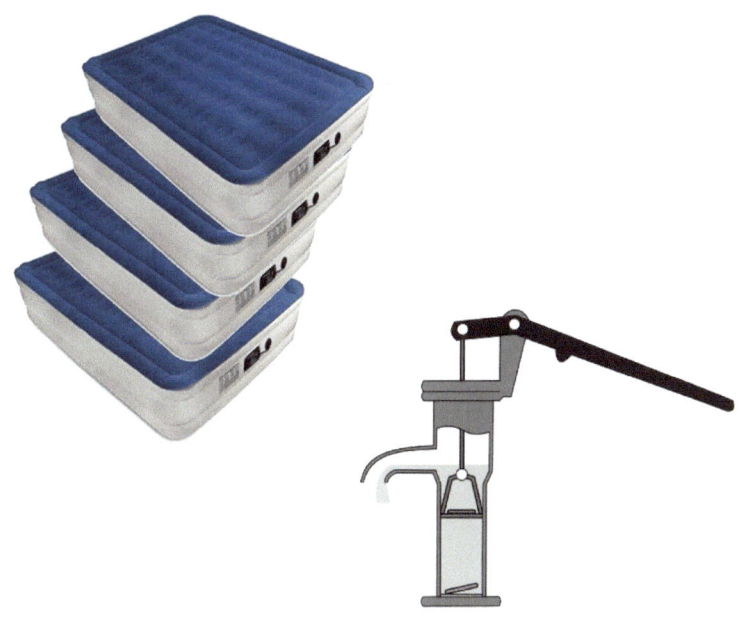

There are many often neglected household items around us that can be used to exchange energy and generate electricity, such as compressed air, pumps and check valves.

百姓日用而不知 . . . 显诸仁，藏诸用，鼓万物而不与圣人同忧

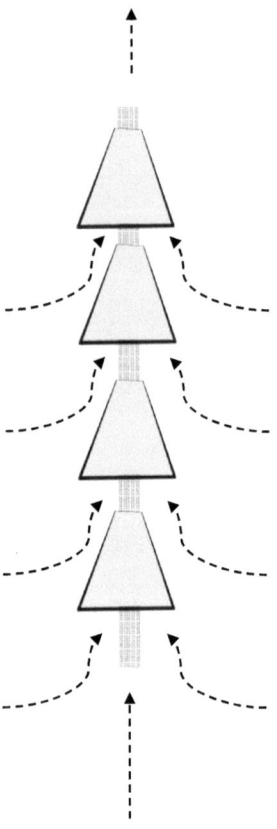

Like buoyance in the water, there is always levity in the air

虽然常被忽略,空气中处处像水中一样有浮力。

Items on the menu if you imagine Empty Air Clean Energy LLC (EACEL) is a fast food franchise
如果空气能源净化公司是一个快餐店的话，会有以下这么一个菜单。

(depending on availability of materials in each household, customers can pick which configuration they want to have installed for their DIY projects, and EACEL will provide help with advice and consultation)
(根据各家情况和条件不同，您可以任选一种模式建筑施工。"空气能源净化公司"将会为您提供咨询和帮助。)

Tai Chi L-U loop

泰祺乾坤圈

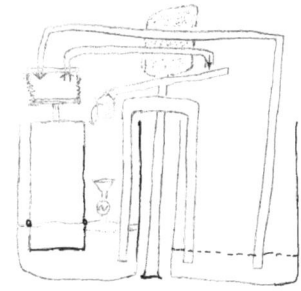

Tai Chi cyclone

泰祺旋

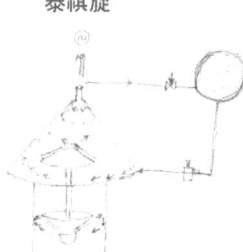

Tai Chi Chamber

泰祺腔

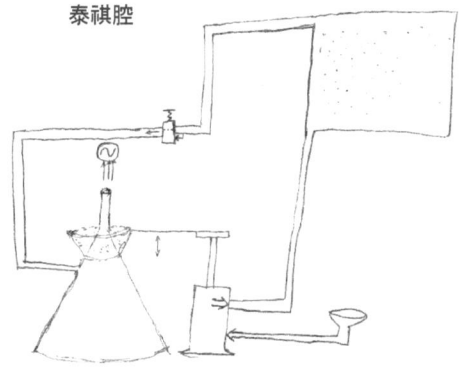

Energy is everywhere

e=mc² : wherever there's mass (fermion), there's energy

e=hν: wherever there's change, there's energy, even with emptiness (like photon, a type of massless boson particle)

The greatest 20th century discoveries in physics are: relativity and quantum mechanics.

二十世纪科学的进步使人类意识到：我们周围能量无处不在。相对论和量子力学告诉我么，1）有质量就有能量；2) 有变化就有能量。

合抱之木生于毫末
九筑之台起于垒土
千里之行始于足下

And now, we are we already living in 21st century. How come we are still not feeling "energy is everywhere around us"?
Not so fast, take a careful look at siphoning. Movements of water and wind can happen anywhere in nature as long as there's air.
  Siphoning of water?
  How about siphoning of air?
What is the driving force of siphoning? Force times distance is energy. Where did the energy come from and where did it go?

生活在二十一世纪，为什么我们还是没有感觉到"能量在我们身边无所不在"？

等会儿，想想"虹吸","呼吸"等等这些现象，又会觉得"呼风唤雨"的能量在我们的周围像空气一样无孔不入，与"空气"同在。这样的能量交换往往在日常生活中被忽视。

是什么力量推动了我们身边的"呼"和"吸"。这样的能量从哪里来，又向哪里去？

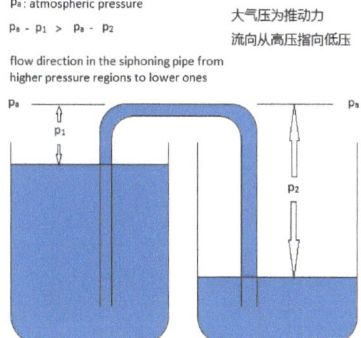 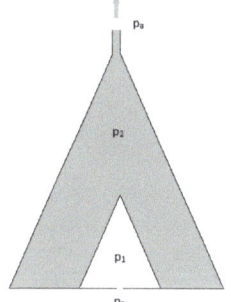

Relativity theory and quantum mechanics are leading mankind to a grand unified theory: all kinds of driving forces (gravity, electromagnetic, strong & weak forces) are "inertial forces", "fictitious forces", "force derived from shifting of reference frame sets", therefore source of all forms of energy are potential energy (products from the dual vector space of: force & distance, or potential & movement, or direction & flow, or voltage & current).

"Fictitious force" or "inertial force" is the force of "self-preservation" or commonly phrased as "self wanting to be self". From the word 自然, "nature" to the concept of "conatus" (Descartes, Spinoza), "inertia" (Galileo, Newtonian 1st law), and "first law of thermodynamics" (a.k.a. conservation of energy), all these important ideas are describing one simple truth, that is universal among all beings: A=A, the identity equation. Within a group, "self wants to be self" can generate forces to "attract" or "repel" between particles, depending on viewing from different reference frames of "in" or "out" (Views of: gravity, electromagnetic, strong/weak forces by General theory of relativity and Group Theory). Everything in the universe are trying to act upon the principle of "self-preservation".

The tendency for the atmosphere to stay stagnant can be cited as a major reason why it is hard to generate wind within an indoor confined environment. In the meantime, shifting the reference between "in" and "out" - the two frame sets, the "tendency" "potential" or the "inertness" for the atmosphere trying to stay static in a large open system is, in fact, the force to propel air molecules traveling between two smaller open systems.

相对论和量子力学正在把人类带向一个大统一理论的时代，所谓"大统一"就是一个使人们意识到宇宙中所有的"力"（重力，电磁力，强相互作用力，弱相互作用力）都是"惯性力"-"虚构的力""坐标系/参照系变换产生的力"的认知。所以一切形式的能量归根结底都是"势能"（产生于对偶的向量空间： 力量/距离；势差/运动；方向/流体；电压/电流 - 的乘积）。

"想象的力"或"惯性力"是一种"自我维护"的力。 这种力通俗的理解是："我是我"，"你是你"或"自己是自己"的力。无论是中文中的"自然"这个词，还是英文中的"nature"或是拉丁语中的"connatus"（笛卡尔，斯宾诺莎时代的用语）以及"惯性"（伽利略的斜面实验，匀速直线运动，牛顿第一定律）， 还有热力学第一定律（封闭体系内能量守恒），都是在描述宇宙中一个简单明了的真理，那就是万事万物都存在一个恒等式的趋势：A=A，"自己是自己"，"自然"。 在一个群体中，"自己是自己"的力量可以在单体之间产生"吸引力"或"排斥力"。产生哪一种力取决于是从"内部"还是"外部"不同的参照系/坐标系的变化（广义相对论，群论对：重力，电磁力，强相互作用力，弱相互作用力， 的看法和理解）。 所有的事和物在宇宙中都在坚持着"自己是自己" - "自我维护" - "自然"。

室内的空气在大气圈中维持现状的"惯性"倾向，对于想在室内产生"风"的实验者来说既可以起到"阻碍"作用，也可以起到"推动"作用。 最后"惯性力"和"势能"起到哪种作用取决于, 如何变换地看待和利用坐标系和参照系: 是把室内环境当成一个大的体系, 还是当成内部有多个小的可以互相流通的开放体系

反者道之动
弱者道之用
有生于无

L'imagination gouverne le monde

天下万物生于有

Continuing with the thoughts about "relativity" and "quantum mechanics" . . .

Relatively big/small - scaling something to a larger or smaller size than they appear, time dilation & distance contraction

Quantum scope - studying the quantum state of some objects in a macro or micro world

There is no reason that prevents anybody from reproducing or simulating circulation of the atmospheric recycling process in a room with inertial forces, that is:

    Use siphoning to construct waterfalls and dams in a household

    Use siphoning to construct wind and draughts in a household

Spirit soars, impurity falls, circular loops facilitate continuous exchange of energy. In the bra-ket notation, a quantum state always has dual vector spaces. Only when both are present, can the description of the field of a force be complete. Then, can energy exchange take place sustainably. Gravitational field forms gravity and levity; Electromagnetic force requires circuit to conduct; Particles in the universe use fission and fusion to complete a cycle of matters and facilitate lasting energy exchange.

话说 "相对论" 和 "量子力学" 包涵着以下的概念和现象：

相对大小 - 将某事某物放得很大，缩得很小， 例如： 坐标系之间的 络仑滋变换使得时间变长，距离变短

量子规模 - 研究宏观和微观世界物质量子状态的变化

在大范围，自然界中，大气圈内水和空气被惯性力推动而循环的现象，完全可以在小范围的室内环境用实验重复，产生和证实。

    在室内空间，虹吸现象中"吸"进来的空气可以推动水像在瀑布中一样往下落。

    虹吸现象中"吸"进来的空气拥有的大气压差也可以推动气体分子形成对流，吹风。

轻气上升，浊气下降，闭合回路，完整的循环产生不断的能量交换。 在狄拉克标注符号中一个量子的状态中有两个"对偶"的向量空间来表述。只有当无独有偶的"来"和"去"两个方向的场都具备以后，才能有可持续的能量交换。例如重力场中有"自由落体"和"上升浮力"两个方向；电磁场形成电路需要有联接 "+" 和 "-" 的著名的"闭合回路"；微观的基本粒子在宇宙的循环中通过"强相互作用力"和" 弱相互作用力"以"聚变"和"裂变"的对偶的形式交换物质和能量。

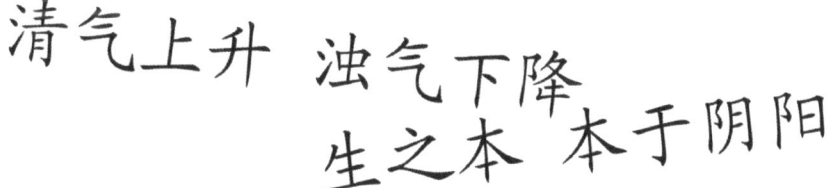

Speaking of "potential", "direction", "tendency" or "field" between water and air, it's almost always easier for water to displace air, than for the opposite to happen, due to the differences in density. Whether for water flowing down a cliff, or for water flowing up into suction as in siphoning, the boundary during the interaction between water and air is like a capacitor in the electronic circuit that can store potential energy.

When we can successfully simulate the nature, and reproduce the process of converting potential energy into kinetic or electrical energy at a large or small scale, outdoor or indoor, Voila! We can have a power station almost anywhere, because air is practically omnipresent.

说到水和空气的界面之间的 "势", "方向", "倾向" 和 "场", 由于有密度的差别, 几乎总是能观察到, 水有序, 有组织地推走空气比空气推走水更自然。不管是水在瀑布中往下, 还是在虹吸系统中往上流, 水和空气的界面的分子之间就像电路中的电容一样储藏着"势能"。

当自然界中大规模地将势能转换成动能或电能的过程能够被成功地被重演和模仿出来的时候, 那么无论是大规模还是小规模, 也无论是室内还是室外, 就有能源了。因为大气圈相对于人类的现实生活几乎可以说是无处不在的。

where theres a hope theres a will
where theres a will theres a way

Tai Chi L-U loop (using water as working fluid)
泰祺乾坤圈 （以水为工作液）

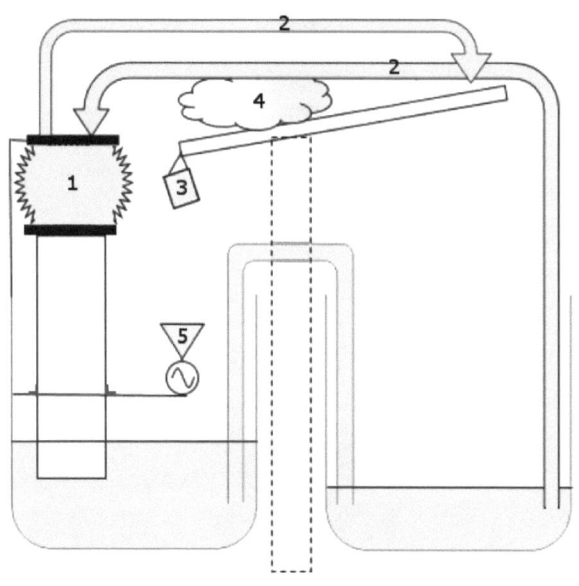

Explanations

1. Pump: in accordion, or other styles
2. Conduits with check valves to direct water flow
3. Tipping/tilting bucket to provide change - rhythm - frequency (as in $e=h\nu$), serve as a pacemaker
4. Water reservoir/sponge/absorbent (to hold water flow just as capacitor to electric flow). To slow the velocity for water falling down has the equivalent effect of increasing the potential energy by raising water level up
5. A funnel shaped container to increase the water pressure propelling the generator

Other parts are self-explanatory

注释

1. 水泵: 风箱或其他式样
2. 装有单向阀的管道
3. 间歇流容器，产生变化，节奏，频率（能量=常数 X 频率）如同起搏器
4. 微型水库/海绵/吸水物（在此储藏水流如同在电路中用电容蕴藏电流一样）。减慢水往下流的速度，相当于往上抬升水位，增加势能
5. 漏斗形容器，在水流过发电机前集中压力

其它部件功能不言自明

Scholium

Just like in the work of respiratory and cardiovascular systems, energy within the air movements from atmosphere to body fluid cannot be generated, but only exchanged.

High pressure areas (such as lung) and check valves (pulmonary and tricuspid valves) and multiple chambers (from fish to reptiles to mammals, number of chambers kept on increasing along evolution lines) are the critical parts that facilitate effective energy exchange.

学术理论

如同在呼吸系统和心血管系统中，空气从大气到液体推动过程中的能量传导机制一样，能量不能凭空产生，只能在不同体系中被交换。

高压区域（如：肺），单向阀（半月瓣，三尖瓣）以及多个的腔，房，室等容器（在动物进化的漫长过程中，从鱼，爬行动物到哺乳动物，心脏逐渐地由两个腔室增加到了四个）组成了有效地推动能量交换的重要部件。

Tai Chi Chamber
泰祺腔

(uses air as working agent, works well in arid regions - to power dehumidifier and generate water)

（**以空气**为传动体，适用于干燥地区，连接吸湿机以产生适量可用水）

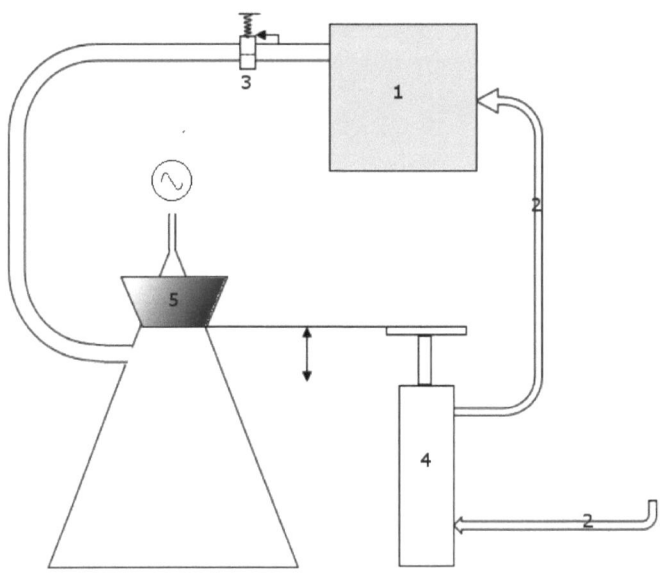

Explanations

1. Compressed air
2. Air ducts with check valves
3. Air pressure regulator
4. Air pump (could be multiple connected in parallel)
5. Weight to squeeze the chamber and push air out

Other parts are self-explanatory

解释

1. 压缩空气
2. 装有单向阀的空气管道
3. 气压控制器
4. 气泵(可以多个并联)
5. 压码,挤压气腔,吹风

其它部件功能不言自明

Scholium

The energy exchange among multiple containers from low to high pressures, and with help of check valves, can happen without involvement of fluid. The drawback of such a device is its relatively low energy output in terms of horsepower or wattage.
The advantage of such a device is that it will be easy to build and applicable in a wide range of areas and under harsh conditions.

学术理论

通过多个容器,不同压差,**再加上**单向阀引导的能量交换可以在不用液体为动力传导介质的条件下, **以空气**为推动媒体进行。 这样的装置**的**

缺点是:**功率**输出会相对小一些。

优点是:容易建造,而且使用环境和区域会广一些。

Tai Chi Dual Cyclone
泰祺旋
(using both air and water as working agents)

（以空气和水为传动物质）

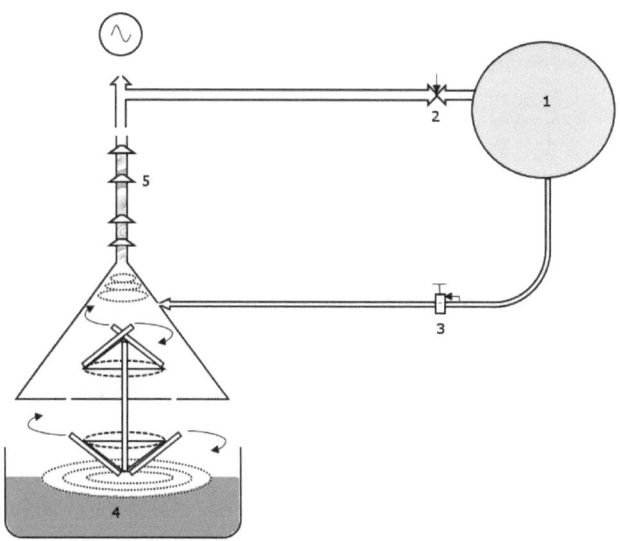

Explanations
1. Compressed air
2. Needle valve
3. Air pressure regulator
4. Water
5. Morphed suction chimney

Other parts are self-explanatory

注释

1. 压缩空气
2. 气针，增压阀
3. 气压控制器
4. 水
5. 改装烟囱，吸管

其它部件功能不言自明

Scholium

Putting it together, there's another kind of energy source that accompany humanity everywhere, all the time, yet often gets neglected. That is the energy derived from the rotation of the earth. With energy sources from "chimney effect", "breathing" and "cyclone/whirlpool" every household is submersed in unlimited amount of energy, even though these forms of energy are hard to be extracted with existing technology, or with small scale naturally formed structures.

But like hydraulic power station, generator, or even bronze, iron, steel before them, human history is filled with man-made new materials being built into artificial structures or devices to gradually blaze the trail, exchanging naturally existing energy in the world more and more effectively. New devices would be invented one day, and that day could not have come sooner.

学术理论

汇总一下， 还有一种一直伴随人类的能源那就是地球自传带来的能量. 。这**种能源也是无**处不在但却常被人们忽视。 当我们考虑到"**烟囱效应**"，"**呼吸**"和"**自然漩涡**"**的推**动力来源之后，就会意识到地球上的每家每户都沉浸在取之不尽用之不竭的能源中。 **但是**这些不易察觉的能量很难用已有的工艺开发，也没有天然形成的材料和小规模结构启示我们如何利用这些能源。转念想一想，水电站，发电机，还有人类历史中更早出现的青铜，铁，钢材不都记载着从自然材料和自然结构中渐渐演化出来了人工材料及用其建造的人工结构，帮助人们更有效地交换能源的发展史吗？ **开采身**边弥漫着的能源的新发明迟早会出现，都生活在了二十一世纪的我们，会觉得越早越好。

Above, we have sketched out several devices and mechanisms capable of extracting potential energy from atmosphere around us. Such energy sources are often ignored but have always being virtually everywhere on earth, professing themselves as in: "chimney effect", "breathing" or "rotating frame sets". These ideas are far from complete or optimally efficient, but it's a start.

Perpetual machines are impossible to build. But less than "perpetual" is quite an achievement nevertheless. What does 24-hour power generation mean to you, even with a few minutes each day to push-forward and maintain?

24 hours/day x 30 days/month = 720 hours per month

Suppose you can build one 1000 watts device, then each month you would have generated 720,000 watts hours or 720 kWH of energy. Check your electric bill. . . that should be enough for most average household. If one unit is not enough, then build another set of 1000 watt units. After all, the energy is from empty air, therefore should be practically inexhaustible.

以上我们勾划了几种从大气中开发被人们忽视，但是却在地球上随时随地都存在的势能的方法。这些能源能在"烟囱效应"，"呼吸"和地球自转引起的各种"旋"中观察到。我们列举的方法在空气能的开发事业中很不完全，离优化和高效的目标也还差得很远。只是在此抛砖引玉。

永动机是不可能造出来的。但是退一步想 24 小时机，需要每天花几分钟助推和维护的 24 小时机，对你意味着什么呢？

24 小时/天 X 30 天/月 = 720 小时 / 月

如果您能造一台 1000 瓦特的装置的话，每个月您就可以发电 720 千瓦时。。。。。。看看您的月电费账单，对一般家庭来说的话 720 千瓦时应该够用了。如果还不够的话，再加造 1000 瓦的一个机组。想一想您的能量来源是"空气"，这样的资源从实际应用上说是取之不尽的。

陰陽不測之謂神

一陰一陽之謂道繼之者善也成之者性也
仁者見之謂之仁知者見之謂之知
百姓日用而不知故君子之道鮮矣
顯諸仁藏諸用鼓萬物而不與聖人同憂盛德大業至矣哉
富有之謂大業日新之謂盛德生生之謂易
成象之謂乾效法之謂坤極數知來之謂占通變之謂事

When random air "bubbles" are scattered in a room, they are just trash. When they are organized, they can become "compressed air". And organized air movements begat more organized air movements. Come to think of it, this is also a form of "self preservation" or "inertial force".

人能群 。 。 。和则一,一则多力,多力则强,强则胜物.

www.ingramcontent.com/pod-product-compliance
Lightning Source LLC
Chambersburg PA
CBHW041757040426
42446CB00001B/65